Daily Readings
with
Blaise Pascal

The Daily Readings Series
Titles now available

Blaise Pascal

Daily Readings
with
Blaise Pascal

edited by
Robert Van de Weyer

Templegate Publishers
Springfield, Illinois

First published in the United States in 1995 by
Templegate Publishers
302 East Adams Street
P.O. Box 5152
Springfield,Illinois 62705

ISBN 0-87243-212-2
Library of Congress Catalog Card Number
95-60057

CONTENTS

The marks of God
Natural faith
Drifting downstream
Freedom of Spirit
Simplicity and charity
The paradox of Christianity
Receiving and losing
True conversion
Reason, habit, inspiration
It is incomprehensible
An astonishing faith

5. REASON

The wager
The truth of religion
Faith and proof
Reason alone
The skeptic's dilemma
Religion and skepticism
Reason and mystery
Useless proofs
The web of doubt
Divine contradictions
The prospect of immortality
The heart's reasons
Unreasonable things
The idol of truth
The gentle way

INTRODUCTION

When he died in 1662, Blaise Pascal was famous as a mathematician and scientist. He had made huge advances in probability theory, virtually creating from nothing a new branch of mathematics. His experiments concerning the vacuum and atmospheric pressure were hailed as a model of the new scientific method. And he had designed the first calculating machine that actually worked. As a religious figure, however, he was still obscure. A polemical work, *Provincial Letters*, in which he sought to defend a friend who was charged with heresy, had made a considerable impact; but, he had written it anonymously. And his greatest work, *Pensees*, had not yet been published.

Today his scientific work is largely forgotten, his achievements having long since been surpassed. In this sphere he is remembered only by schoolchildren as the inventor of "Pascal's triangle." But in the field of religion and spirituality, he must rank as one of the best-known and widely-read authors of all time. Moreover as a Roman Catholic he has enjoyed equal appeal amongst Protestants, ever since John

Wesley warmly praised his short essay on conversion.

Blaise Pascal was born on 19 June 1623 in Clermont-Ferraud, where his father was the legal officer. His mother died when he was aged three, and in 1631 the family moved to Paris. His father directed his education. Despite demanding the highest standards, his father failed to provide him with adequate books. Nonetheless by the age of twelve he had discovered for himself the mathematical propositions of Euclid. Deprived both of maternal affection and the friendship of other boys, young Blaise was delicate both mentally and physically. He was tense and inhibited, subject to bouts of depression, and expressed shock when his elder sister, Gilberthe, embraced and kissed her small children. And, by his own testimony, he felt perpetually ill, often resorting to his bed.

In 1640, at the age of 17, Pascal published his first mathematical work, an essay on conic sections. It was widely admired, and he found himself hailed as a mathematical genius. For the next six years he was almost wholly engaged in further scientific research. Like his father he was devout, attending Mass each Sunday and observing all the festivals and fasts; but there was no fervour in his faith and, as he later recognized, he kept his religion and daily life in quite separate compartments. But in 1646 Pascal made contact with a religious group, known as the Jansenists, whose rigorous teaching and intense spirituality was to dominate the rest of his life.

The young Pascal lived almost entirely through his intellect, his mind absorbed by mathematics. But as he grew to maturity he was beset by intense emotions. In an early essay, entitled *On the Passion of Love,* we see him struggling to reconsider emotion and intellect — or, as he puts it, "love" and "ambition."

The Jansenists, named after their founder, Jansenius, taught that personal conversion was essential for salvation. Though strict Roman Catholics, they shared the Protestant belief that outward observance of religious rules could never save the individual soul. This could only be achieved by an unmerited act of grace, in which God infuses the soul with his love. Once a person has been saved he will reject worldly ambition and wealth, and devote his entire energies to the service of God. To the lonely and anguished heart of Pascal such a warm faith had an overwhelming appeal. He continued his scientific work, but spent much of his time at Port Royal, the convent in Paris which was the center of Jansenist activity.

Pascal loved the convent worship, and his intellectual outlook was transformed by Jansenist theology. But for eight years he could find no spiritual peace, and he began to despair of ever experiencing the personal conversion for which he yearned. Then on the night of 23 November 1654 he experienced two hours of intense joy in which he felt drawn into direct contact with God. Immediately afterwards he wrote down his *Memorial* in which he recorded his reaction. It is garbled, even confused, and for that reason has the ring of authenticity which more sober accounts of personal conversion often lack. *The Memorial* is an astonishing testimony to the power of God over a human soul. It is an outburst of love and praise, a piece of spontaneous poetry in which logic is overwhelmed by passionate joy. He sewed it into the lining of his jacket so that he could always wear it next to his heart and there it was found at his death.

The remaining eight years of his life were devoted entirely to sharing the joy and insight which he had received. Soon after his conversion, Pascal attempted to stand back from his experience and analyze it. He describes the different psychological stages leading up to and following the experience of conversion in a short essay on the psychology of conversion, which a century later so deeply impressed John Wesley, the founder of Methodism. And he composed a most moving set of prayers for those who are sick, in which the sickness itself is accepted as a gift from God. But his grandest project, undertaken at the instigation of the priests of Port Royal, was *An Apology for the Christian Religion,* to be addressed to skeptics. He wrote down many short paragraphs, aphorisms, and even entire essays in preparation for the work. And he assembled these into sections.

But by 1659 his health began to deteriorate, so that work on the project was virtually abandoned. Pascal said that he never passed a day without suffering. Some have speculated that he had tuberculosis, which lasted many years and probably eventually killed him. He also seems to have suffered acute nervous tension. He came to regard sickness as a blessing through which God draws the human heart to himself. He entitled these meditations, *Prayer to Ask of God the Good Use of Sickness*. On 19 August 1662 he died, probably from a combination of tuberculosis and stomach cancer. His friends attempted to complete his project, making use of the papers he had left; and eight years after his death the first, rather muddled version appeared. It was not until 1844, however, that an authentic edition was published under the title *Pensées (Thoughts)*, in which Pascal's manuscript was printed virtually unaltered. It is on this extraordinary collection of ideas and insights that his growing reputation is based.

The starting point of Pascal's philosophy is that all people seek happiness. The case for Christianity must therefore depend on whether it brings happiness. To Pascal it was self-evident that the pursuit of material pleasures is ultimately unsatisfying; and as he looked at the world around him he saw misery and despair in people's hearts. He himself had only found happiness after his conversion in 1654, and thereafter he dedicated himself to showing that the Christian faith can bring the same joy to everyone.

Pascal as a religious writer is impossible to categorize. He was not a theologian. Yet he applied his logical scientific mind to theological issues, and was profoundly concerned with the relationships between faith and reason. His greatest desire was to show that the Christian faith accords with reason, so it is in the nature of man to accept it. This view is expressed most clearly in his famous metaphor of *The Wager*. But he also recognized the limits of reason; that there were mysteries which faith alone could fathom. And he acknowledged that many people, who claim to reject faith on rational grounds, are actually swayed by their own irrational passions. He was not a mystic. Yet he had a quirky, almost perverse spiritual imagination which flashed rays of light into the dark corners of the human soul. Pascal was an acute observer of the human condition. And many of his aphorisms have become a familiar part of our mental furniture. Occasionally he can seem slightly glib, as if he is impressed by his own wit. But he hits the mark with an unerring accuracy; and it is clear that Pascal himself is his own target. Although not a master of prayer, he was fervent in his devotion to Christ. The word that leaps most readily to mind is 'Genius'; one is here in the presence of a unique religious intelligence.

The

emorial

THE MEMORIAL

In the year of grace 1654, on Monday 23 November, feast of Saint Clement, pope and martyr…From about half past ten in the evening until about half past midnight.

FIRE

"God of Abraham, God of Isaac, God of Jacob," not of the philosophers and scholars.
Certainty. Certainty. Emotion. Joy. Peace.
God of Jesus Christ.
"My God and your God."
Your God shall be my God.
Forgetting the world and all things, except only God. He can be found only by the ways taught in the Gospel.
Greatness of the human soul.
Righteous Father, the world has not known you, but I have known you.
Joy, joy, joy, tears of joy.
I have cut myself off from him.
"They have forsaken me, the fountain of living water."
"My God, will you forsake me?"
May I not be cut off from him for ever!

"This is life eternal, that they know you, the only true God, and Jesus Christ, whom you have sent."

Jesus Christ.

Jesus Christ.

I have cut myself off from him, shunned him, decried him, crucified him.

Let me never be cut off from him!

We cling to him only by the ways taught in the Gospel.

Sweet and total renunciation.

Total submission to Jesus Christ and to my director.

Eternal joy in return for one day's trial on earth.

"I will not forget your word."

Amen.

onversion

CONFUSION

When God is pleased to enter into intimate communion with the soul, his first action is to bestow an extraordinary knowledge and insight, through which the soul reflects on itself and on the world in a way that is altogether new. The enlightenment instills a holy fear, which stirs up in the soul a profound regret at all the years that have been wasted in idle pleasures. The soul now finds it can no longer enjoy these old pleasures, and even the thought of them causes unease. Yet paradoxically the soul also feels a strange aversion to the invisible, spiritual joys of God. This is because the old visible pleasures, which still seem attractive as well as repulsive, are in direct opposition to the new invisible joys; and the only way the soul can escape this conflict is to turn inside for every form of joy. The soul thus finds itself in deep confusion and perplexity.

ASTONISHMENT

The soul soon recognizes that many of its attachments are destined to pass away: its own mind and body; relatives and friends; possessions and reputation; authority and status; health, and even life itself. And it realizes that all these mortal, perishable things cannot satisfy its deepest desires, for the soul yearns for a stable, unchanging condition of bliss that will last for all eternity. The soul then feels astonished that for so long it had been blind to the mortality of her attachments, and blind to her own true needs. And she is astonished at how so many other people in the world are also blind. Thus to the initial confusion is added astonishment. The fact that such blindness is so common sows the seed of doubt, in which the soul wonders whether such perishable attachments are in fact the only source of pleasure, and thus the new insights are illusory. But then the soul remembers that everyone eventually discovers that worldly pleasures are mere dust, as health and life slip away.

SILENCE

The soul now turns all her powers to the search for true goodness. And she realizes that true goodness must contain certain properties. It must be durable, like the soul herself. It must be secure, unable to be lost. And it must be so precious that the soul can conceive nothing more precious. The soul then concludes that God alone contains these properties; that nothing is worthy of the fullness of love other than God himself, who created love. The soul now rejoices that she has found true goodness that cannot be taken away from her. And she begins to contemplate the Creator in a state of profound humility and heartfelt adoration. She is conscious that in the presence of God she is as nothing. Nor can she form any clear idea of true goodness, since God in his glory is so far above her own experience. So she gives up trying to think about God, and now simply rests in his presence. Silence becomes her most natural form of prayer, since words and ideas can have so little grasp on the mystery of God.

HUMILITY

The soul now realizes that she has embarked on a journey without knowing the way. So, in all humility, she turns to God, praying that, since he has been pleased to show himself to her, he will also guide her towards him. She asks God to be both the destination of her journey, and the companion who shows her the route. But God does not himself offer a guiding hand. Instead he prompts her to do what travelers on an earthly journey have to do: to ask other travelers, more familiar with the landscape, to give directions. Now the soul is compelled to swallow all pride, and ask for the spiritual course of fellow travelers.

RESOLUTION

The soul makes a firm resolution that for the rest of her life on earth she will live in conformity with God's will. But the weakness of her human nature, and her tendency to fall back into those sins in which she formerly lived, mean that by herself she cannot keep the first resolution. So she makes a second resolution; to pray constantly to God to give her the strength to keep the first resolution in the way the soul acknowledges that it is her duty to worship God, since she is his creation; to give thanks to God, since he is the source of all joy; to see forgiveness for her persistent weakness; and to beg earnestly for his strength.

assion

TWO GREAT PASSIONS

The passions most common in man, and which give birth to many others, are love and ambition. They have no necessary connection with each other, yet they are often found united. Their tendency, however, is to weaken, and even to destroy, each other. Even the greatest mind can only be under the sway of one great passion at a time. When, therefore, love and ambition are found united they exercise only a divided power over the soul, compared with that which would be exercised by either of them alone. Their sway is not limited by years: youth and old age both feel their influences. They spring up in the morning of life, and wither only in the grave.

THE COURSE OF LIFE

Life is happiest if it starts with love, and ends with ambition. If I could make the choice, that is what I would prefer for myself. As long as the vital warmth of youth continues, man loves. But that fire gradually subsides, and is extinguished. It should then be gracefully and nobly replaced by ambition. By ambition I mean mental stimulation, an ardent desire to discern the truth, a delight in spiritual insight. In this way the ambitious man is preparing for death, when truth shall be fully revealed.

PURITY OF SPIRIT

Purity of spirit produces corresponding purity of passion. Thus a pure and elevated mind loves with the greatest intensity. And a pure and elevated mind is also most ardent for truth. Pure love expresses itself in generous action. Pure ambition for truth expresses itself in profound imagination.

SEARCH FOR BEAUTY

We are born with a propensity to love, and with a desire for truth. Love will naturally seek many objects, looking always for that which is beautiful — including sexual beauty in those of the opposite gender. But the soul should eventually look at itself for the greatest beauty. This is because each person is created in God's image and so is infinitely beautiful; and since the individual knows himself best of all, he should seek God's beauty through introspection. By this means, the search for love is transformed into the search for truth, because the divine truth is to be found in every soul.

TRANSFORMING LOVE

Love gives birth to qualities which did not exist before. A mean man becomes generous. A greedy man enjoys sharing his wealth. A cold man without compassion becomes warm and hospitable. A man who is introspective, unable to express emotion, finds his heart breaks free as love flows out from it. Often people condemn love as irrational, and so are afraid of its power to transform people. Even poets sometimes claim that love is blind. But love and reason, far from opposing one another, should be regarded as complementary. The passion of love opens a person's eyes, enabling him to see the full beauty of God's creation. Reason then gives form and meaning to what he sees, convincing him that God is indeed the author of all things.

aith

FALSE PURSUIT OF HAPPINESS

All men seek happiness. There are no exceptions. Although they may use different methods, their goal is the same. Some may go to war while others stay at home; but their basic desire is the same, even though it may be interpreted differently. Happiness is the motive of every act of every man, including those who go and hang themselves. Yet for very many years no one without faith has ever reached the goal at which everyone is continually aiming. All men complain: princes, nobles, commoners, old, young, strong, weak, learned, ignorant, healthy, sick. In every country, at every time, all sorts and conditions, they complain. By now, after such a long experience, without pause or charge, we ought to be convinced that we cannot attain happiness by our own efforts. But experience serves to teach us little. Since no two examples are exactly alike, we convince ourselves that our particular case is different, deluding ourselves that we will not suffer the same disappointment as everyone before us has suffered.

FOOTPRINTS OF HAPPINESS

The fact that all men pursue happiness should convince us that happiness is possible. It is as if the footprint and trace of some past era of happiness is still on our souls. The one who left that footprint is God. God alone is man's true happiness. Since man abandoned God, man has found nothing to take his place: stars, sky, earth, elements, plants, animals, war, vice, adultery, incest. Since losing the true source of goodness, man has looked for goodness in all things, and has been disappointed in every case. But some have realized that happiness, desired by everyone, cannot lie in any of the particular things which individuals crave. They have understood that happiness cannot be based on external objects which an individual can possess, such as wealth or power, since their possession by one individual causes grief and envy in others. This realization is the beginning of faith, since it teaches that happiness must transcend the things of creation, and must therefore be with their Creator.

MAN'S GREATNESS

Man's greatness comes from knowing that he is wretched. A tree does not know that it is wretched. One must feel wretched to know that one is wretched. But that knowledge raises man above the trees.

THE REQUIREMENTS OF TRUE RELIGION

The greatness of man, and also his wretchedness, are so evident that the true religion must teach us both the source of greatness and the source of wretchedness. And it must account for the amazing contradiction between these two principles. It must show that a God exists whom we are bound to love; that our true bliss is to be found in him, and our sole cause of misery is to be cut off from him. It must acknowledge that we are full of darkness which prevents us from knowing and loving him. It must then show why we turn away from God, and thus away from the bright light of our own happiness. Finally it must teach us the cure for this miserable condition, and show us the means of obtaining that cure.

GOD THROUGH CHRIST

We know God only through Jesus Christ. Without this mediator, all communication with God is broken off. Through Jesus we know God. All those who have claimed to know God and prove his existence are deluded, their proofs futile and worthless. But to prove Christ we have the ancient prophecies which foretold his coming, and which were verified by events. Thus these prophecies have been shown to be reliable, and these prove that Jesus is divine. Yet even this is not sufficient. We must also acknowledge our own wretchedness, and hence cry out to Jesus as our redeemer. Indeed, those who know God in Jesus, but do not know their own wretchedness, and hence do not accept Jesus as their redeemer, will not glorify God, but will glorify themselves.

THE MARKS OF GOD

Let man contemplate the whole of nature in her majestic glory. Let him look up to the sun, the magnificent source of all warmth and light, and let him acknowledge this earth as a mere speck in the vast universe. Let him remember that nature is an infinite sphere, whose center is everywhere and whose circumference is nowhere. Let him then look upon the smallest insect he can find, and wonder at the infinite complexity of this creature's body, with minute legs and head. And then let him realise that nature is not only infinitely large, but also infinitely small, with each atom containing within itself a universe of smaller entities. And finally let him acknowledge that the Creator has left his mark on all things, from the dazzling sun to the tiny insect.

NATURAL FAITH

Those who believe Christianity without having read the Bible do so because they are already holy in spirit. So everything they hear about Christianity echoes within their breast. They feel that God made them, and their natural desire is to love God. They feel that they are not strong enough to go to God on their own to ask for his love, and that by themselves they cannot pray to him. So when they hear that God made himself man in order to unify himself with all humanity, they are overjoyed, immediately welcoming Jesus as their saviour.

DRIFTING DOWNSTREAM

Man can have neither certain knowledge nor total ignorance. We are like boats on a great river, drifting downstream, not knowing our destination. We look for clear truths that we can cling to, like old trees sticking above the water, hoping that we can then stop and rest. But as soon as we try to grasp at a branch it slips in our hands, and we continue onwards. We cannot stand still. Movement is our natural state, but is contrary to our most ardent desire. We yearn to tie our boat to a firm rock, but we are never near enough to the bank to throw a rope. Yet although we do not know our destination, we can see guidance and protection on our journey, so that we shall arrive there safely. Our destination is God whom we cannot know; but he is also our guide and protector, and we can pray to him.

FREEDOM OF SPIRIT

I love poverty because Christ loved it. I love riches because they give me the means of helping the poor. I keep faith with everyone. I do not render evil to those who wrong me, but I wish them to share my blessings. I try to be fair, honest, sincere and faithful to all people. I have a tender heart for those to whom God has more closely united me. And when I am alone I am aware that all my actions are in God's sight, who is the judge of all. These are my attitudes. And every day I thank my Redeemer who has planted them in me. He has turned a man, who was the slave of lust and pride, into someone who is free.

SIMPLICITY AND CHARITY

Jesus said great things with such simplicity that he seemed not to have thought about them. Yet he said them with such clarity that they seemed to arise from the deepest thoughts. Such simplicity with such clarity is truly wonderful.

THE PARADOX OF CHRISTIANITY

Christianity is strange. It urges people to regard themselves as vile, even abominable. And then it encourages them to be like God. Without this paradox, man's self-abasement would lead to despair, and his exaltation would produce vanity.

RECEIVING AND LOSING

It is vital that we should recognise that we can not only receive grace, but also lose it. If we imagined we could only receive grace, we would become complacent. If we are obsessed with the possibility of losing grace, we shall go mad with anxiety.

TRUE CONVERSION

Some people say, "If I had seen a miracle, I would be converted." How can they be so sure about their reaction? They imagine that conversion means entering into some kind of bargain with God, in which he performs miracles in exchange for good behavior. True conversion consists in self-annihilation before God, recognizing that we can do nothing without him, and that we have deserved nothing but his anger. It consists in knowing that there is an irreconcilable opposition between God and us, and that only through the mediation of Christ can there be union.

REASON, HABIT, INSPIRATION

There are three ways to believe: reason, habit, inspiration. We should open our minds to all the proofs of Christianity, recognizing that Christianity entirely conforms to reason. And we should reinforce our beliefs through habit, reciting the Creed and listening to sermons. But reason and habit alone can never amount to real faith. It is inspiration which brings arid doctrine to life.

IT IS INCOMPREHENSIBLE

It is incomprehensible that God should exist, and it is incomprehensible that the soul should be joined to the body, and that we should have no soul. It is incomprehensible that the world should be created, and that it should not. It is incomprehensible that human beings should be born sinful, and that they should not.

AN ASTONISHING FAITH

There is no denying it: Christianity seems to me quite astonishing. "It is because you were born into it", people will say. Far from it. I stiffened myself against it for that very reason, for fear of being corrupted by prejudice. Indeed it is surely astonishing that I, who have known the Christian faith since earliest childhood, should find it astonishing.

eason

THE WAGER

Either God exists or he does not exist. But which view should be taken? Reason cannot answer this question. Imagine a coin is being spun which will come down heads or tails; how will you wager? Since a choice must be made, let us see where your real interest lies. You have two things at stake: truth and happiness. What is the gain and the loss if you call heads, that God exists. If you win, you win everything; if you lose, you lose nothing. A gambler, where there is an equal chance of gain or loss, would place a bet if the possible gain was twice the possible loss. but here the possible gain is infinite, and the possible loss nothing. Every gambler takes a certain risk for uncertain gain. Here you are taking a certain risk with the prospect either of infinite gain if you win, or no loss if you lose.

THE TRUTH OF RELIGION

Many people despise religion. They hate it and are afraid that it may be true. The cure for this is first to show that religion does not conflict with reason, but deserves our respect. Then we should make it attractive, so that good people wish that it were true. Finally we should demonstrate that it penetrates the deepest mysteries of the human condition.

FAITH AND PROOF

Faith is different from proof. Proof is human, whereas faith is a gift from God. The apostle Paul says, "The just shall live by faith." This is the faith that God himself puts into our hearts, often using proof as the instrument. The apostle Paul also says, "Faith comes by hearing." This faith in our hearts does not make us say, "I know;" it makes us proclaim, "I believe."

REASON ALONE

Those whose hearts have been moved by God to know the truths of Christ are fortunate. They can rightly feel quite certain of the Gospel. But those whose hearts have not been moved are not denied all truth. By reason alone they can be shown that Christianity is not unreasonable. That in itself will open their hearts to God, so that he can instil faith in his own good time.

THE SKEPTICS' DILEMMA

The strongest of the skeptics' arguments is that religious belief is based only on intuition, and that intuition cannot provide proof. There is no way of proving that man was created by a good God; he may equally have been created by an evil demon, or just by chance. Thus the skeptics insist, everything is open to doubt. But the same applies to our ordinary experience. No one can be sure whether he is sleeping or waking, because when we are dreaming we are firmly convinced that we are awake. Is it not possible, therefore, that our entire life is a dream, from which we will awake when we die? We only distinguish between waking and sleeping, and only assert the objective truth of our waking experiences, by a process of intuition. Is, therefore, a man to doubt everything — to doubt whether he is awake, whether he is being pinched or burned? No one goes as far as that. And so I maintain that a genuine skeptic has never existed.

RELIGION AND SKEPTICISM

Let the skeptics first learn what religion is before attacking it. If religion boasted that it offered a clear vision of God, and if it asserted that there was ample evidence of his existence, then the skeptic could simply argue that the evidence is not conclusive. But religion says the opposite. It recognizes that men are in darkness, remote from God, that he has hidden himself from their understanding. And it proclaims that he has given signs of himself for those who truly seek him with their hearts. Thus the skeptic could only successfully attack Christianity if he himself had sincerely sought God, and failed to find any signs. And there are indeed some people who make this claim, saying that they have studied the Bible in depth. But on closer questioning it turns out that they have spent only a few hours reading the Bible, looking not for truth, but for inconsistencies with which to attack Christianity.

REASON AND MYSTERY

If we try to understand truth by reason alone, our religion will be left with nothing mysterious or supernatural. If we ignore the principles of reason, our religion will be absurd and ridiculous.

USELESS PROOFS

The philosophical proofs for the existence of God are so remote from human experience and so complex that they make little impact. And even if some people were at first convinced by them, impressed by their apparent logic, an hour later they would be filled with doubt, wondering if the proofs contained some logical flaw. The trouble with such an approach to God is that it is based on pride — pride in our own power of reason. Thus what is gained by curiosity is lost through pride. We should have the humility to accept, with glad and joyful hearts, that we cannot know God without knowing Jesus Christ as our friend and saviour.

THE WEB OF DOUBT

I look round in every direction, and all I see is darkness. Nature has nothing to offer me that does not give rise to doubt and anxiety. If I saw no signs of God, I should find some means of living without religion. If I saw signs of God every-where, I should peacefully and joyfully accept religious faith. But in fact there seems so much that denies his existence and so much that affirms it. I have frequently prayed that, if there is a God, he should proclaim himself so forcefully to me that nothing can refute him. Yet also, in my desperation, I have asked that, if there is a God, the apparent signs in nature of divinity should be erased. But neither has occurred, and so I am caught between faith and unfaith — I am caught in a web of doubt, unable to move this way or that.

DIVINE CONTRADICTIONS

We desire truth, and find in ourselves nothing but uncertainty. We seek happiness, and find only misery. We are incapable of not desiring truth and happiness; and yet we are on our own incapable of knowing either truth or happiness. This contradiction which leads me away from religion, is in fact the thing which leads me to true religion.

THE PROSPECT OF IMMORTALITY

The immortality of the soul is something of such vital importance to us, affecting us so deeply, that a person must have lost all feeling not to care about the facts of the matter. All our thoughts and actions must depend on how we regard our prospects after death. Thus our chief interest must be to seek enlightenment on this subject. I make a clear distinction between those who strive with all their might to learn, and those who live without bothering to think about it. I have nothing but compassion for the former, who long to have their doubts transformed into faith. The attitude of the latter, however, astounds and appalls me, not because it is immoral, but because it is so profoundly stupid. After all, in this life there are no solid and lasting pleasures, and there are innumerable causes of suffering. So it is surely reasonable to investigate the claim of Christianity that there can be eternal joy beyond the grave.

THE HEART'S REASONS

The heart has its reasons of which reason knows nothing. I believe it is natural for the heart either to love God or to love itself, according to its choice. If it loves one, it hardens against the other. The heart alone can make that claim, because only the heart can perceive God. That is what we mean by faith: God perceived by the heart, not by reason.

UNREASONABLE THINGS

The most unreasonable things in the world can become the most reasonable because men are so unbalanced. What could be less reasonable than to choose as ruler of a state the eldest son of a king? We do not choose as captain of a ship the most highly born of those on board: that would be ridiculous and unjust. Should we choose as ruler the most virtuous and able person? That would lead to terrible conflict, with everyone claiming to be the most virtuous and able. At least if we choose the king's eldest son there can be no argument. Reason can do no better, because civil war is the greatest of evils.

THE IDOL OF TRUTH

We can make an idol of truth itself. For truth apart
from love is not God, but his image and idol,
which we should neither love nor worship. And
still less should we love and worship its opposite,
falsehood.

THE GENTLE WAY

God wishes us to be gentle with each other. And he wants us to instill religion in the minds of others with sweet and natural argument; and he wants us to instill religion into their hearts by opening their hearts to his grace. But if we seek to instill religion by force and by threats, whether physical or moral, it is not religion they will acquire, but terror.

bservations

CONFESSION

Someone told me that he felt great joy and confidence when he had been to confession. Someone else told me that after confession he still felt afraid of divine punishment for his sins. My reaction was that a good man could be made by putting these two together, for in truth both feelings are appropriate after confession.

VANITY

Vanity is so firmly rooted in man's heart that a soldier, a cook or a porter will boast of their abilities, and yearn for admiration. Even philosophers want people to admire them; even when they write against the folly of human vanity they want to be admired for the style of their prose. And those who read philosophy want to be respected for the depth of their understanding. Perhaps in writing this I too am fishing for the admiration of my readers.

A THINKING REED

Man is a reed, weak and flimsy, tossed to and fro. There is no need for the whole universe to take up arms to crush him; a single wave or a strong wind could blow him over. But man is a thinking reed. Even if the universe were to crush him, he would not lose his dignity, because this depends on the power of thought. It is on thought that we should rely, not physical prowess. Let us strive to think well; and, through good thoughts, act well.

THREE SORTS OF PEOPLE

There are three sorts of people: those who have found God and serve him; those who are seeking God and have not found him; and those who are not seeking him and are not trying to find him. The first are wise and happy. The last are unwise and unhappy. Those in the middle are unhappy and wise.

DIVERSION

If a man were happy, he would not want idle diversions. Does that mean that a man who enjoys diversion is unhappy? Yes, because he is consistently looking outside himself for happiness. Thus he is dependent on the vagaries of his circumstances, always liable to be disturbed by some mishap, which inevitably mars his pleasure.

OUR DOUBLE LIVES

Is it not clear that man has two forms of consciousness, two levels of existence? If man had never been corrupted, he would enjoy perfect truth and happiness. But equally, if he had never known corruption he could not be aware of that truth and happiness — for we know things by experiencing their absence. In this world we are frequently unhappy and wretched; yet we have an inkling of perfect truth and happiness. We have an image of truth, and yet possess nothing but falsehood. We are caught between perfect knowledge and absolute ignorance. We live at one and the same time in two spheres — that of truth and that of falsehood.

PAST, PRESENT, FUTURE

We never keep our minds on the present moment. We remember the past, as if we wanted to slow down the passage of time. And we look forward to the future, as if we wanted time to accelerate. We wander about in times that do not belong to us, and do not think about the only time that does. We dream of times past and future, and flee from the present. The reason is that the present is usually painful. We push it out of sight because it distresses us — only on those few occasions which are truly enjoyable are we sorry to see time slip away. We try to reduce present pain with joyful hopes of the future, planning how we are going to arrange things in a period over which we have no control and which we cannot be sure of reaching... The past and present are our means, and the future alone is our end. Thus we never actually live, but hope to live. We are never actually happy, but are constantly planning how to become happy.

THE VANITY OF LIFE

Anyone who does not see the vanity of the world is very vain himself. So who does not see it? The answer is, people whose lives consist of noisy parties, idle amusements and thoughts for the future. Take away all their diversions, and they would be bored to the point of madness. They would feel the vanity of their lives, without recognizing it. They would find themselves utterly depressed, without the power of introspection to discern the cause.

FUTILITY OF WORK

It amazes me that people are not amazed at their own weakness. People work hard and seriously at their various jobs, not because they have ever asked whether their work is the right thing to do, but out of blind obedience to the dictates of society. Then some of us feel disappointed at the futility of our efforts, blaming ourselves for failing to use our gifts and skills to the best advantage. However, the majority of people never question their work, nor realize that they are slaves to society, ever congratulating themselves on their wisdom and maturity.

FALSE AUTHORITY

Since a king is always accompanied by guards, officers, and drummers, and all the other things that induce fear and respect in people, we tend to fear the king himself. So when we see the king unattended, his face alone is enough to strike fear into our hearts. This is because we make no distinction in our minds between the person and the outward sign of his position. As a result the world imagines that the king's authority derives from some supernatural force, saying "the mark of divinity is stamped upon his character"...In fact the authority of kings is based on the folly of the people; and their power is founded on the mental weakness of their subjects. This, of course, is a remarkably sound foundation, for nothing is more certain than that people will be foolish and weak.

SCIENCE AND MORALITY

Knowledge of physical science will not compensate for ignorance of morality in times of trouble. But knowledge of morality will always uplift me in times of trouble, regardless of my ignorance of physical science.

THE PURPOSE OF THOUGHT

Man is made to think. It is his whole duty and whole dignity. And his purpose is to learn to think as he ought. This means that he should begin by thinking honestly about himself, and end by contemplating this God who created him. What, then, do most people think about? They think about dancing, playing the lute, singing, composing rhymes, playing games. And they think about becoming rich or even becoming a king. But they do not think about what it really means to be a king or to be a man.

UNFATHOMED REASONS

Why is my knowledge limited? Why my stature? Why is the upper limit of my life a hundred years rather than a thousand? What reason has nature for making me as I am, for choosing this number of hairs on my head rather than another number? With an infinity of different possibilities, why is my life as it is?

THE FRAGILITY OF FRIENDSHIP

I wager that, if all men knew what other men were saying about them, there would not be four friends left in the world. This is evident from the quarrels sometimes caused by indiscreet repetition.

TIME HEALS

Time heals our griefs and quarrels because we change: we are no longer the same person. Neither the offended party nor the offender is the person he was. It is the same when nations quarrel. After two generations the quarrel is healed because the nations have changed.

THE INNER VACUUM

Nothing is so unbearable to a man as a condition of complete rest, without passions, without work, without amusements, without any kind of stimulus. It is then that he feels his own nothingness, his loneliness, his powerlessness. He feels a vacuum inside himself. Then from the depths of his soul there well up sadness, melancholy, self-disgust, despair.

ickness

FIRST PRAYER

Lord, you are good and gentle in all your ways; and your mercy is so great that not only the blessings but also the misfortunes of your people are channels of your compassion. Grant that I may turn to you as a Father in my present condition since the change in my own state from health to sickness brings no change to you. You are always the same, and you are my loving Father in times of trouble and in times of joy alike.

SECOND PRAYER

You gave me health that I might serve you; and so often I failed to use my good health in your service. Now you send me sickness in order to correct me. My heart was full of pride and selfish ambition when I was healthy. Now please let sickness destroy that pride and ambition. Render me incapable of enjoying any worldly pleasures, that I may take delight in you alone. Grant that I may adore you in the lonely silence of my sick bed. And grant that, having ignored the things of the spirit when my body was vigorous, I may now enjoy spiritual sweetness while my body groans in pain.

THIRD PRAYER

How happy is the heart, O God, that can love an object so pleasing as yourself, the heart that can find its peace in an object so beautiful. How secure and durable is the happiness that is found in you since you endure for ever. Neither life nor death can separate such happiness from its object. Move my heart, O God, to repentance for all my faults, for all the many times I have looked elsewhere for happiness. Let the disorder in my body be the means through which my soul is put into order. I can now find no happiness in physical things; let me find happiness only in you.

FOURTH PRAYER

You can see me, Lord, as I truly am; and surely you can find nothing pleasing to you in me. I can see in myself, Lord, nothing but my sufferings. Yet I find comfort in the knowledge that, in a small way, these resemble your sufferings. Look down, Lord, on the pains that I suffer, on the illness that afflicts me. Look down, blessed Saviour, on the wounds that your hand has made. You did love your own sufferings, even though they ended in death itself. You became man that you might suffer more than any man has done, in order to save man. In your body you embraced all bodily suffering. Look with favor upon my body, look with love upon my pain. Let my sorrows be my invitation to you to visit me on my sick bed.

FIFTH PRAYER

Uproot in me, Lord the self-pity on which self-love feeds. Let me not dwell with self-pity on my own sufferings. Let me not regret the loss of worldly pleasures; remind me that such pleasures can never satisfy the heart. Clothe my heart in the sorrow that clothed your heart on the cross. Let me henceforth ask for neither health nor life, but rather let me be content to let you dispose of me as you please. Let health and sickness, life and death, be equal in my sight. Let me joyfully acknowledge you as my king, and give and take away your blessings as you wish. Let me trust in your eternal providence, receiving with equal reverence all that comes to me from you.

SIXTH PRAYER

O my Saviour, since I share in some small way
your sufferings, fill me to the brim with the glory
which your sufferings won for mankind. Let me
share in some small way the joy of your risen life.

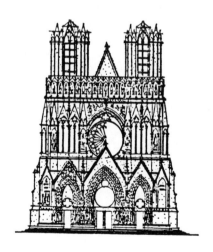

The Modern Spirituality Series

This series, in the same format as this present volume, presents selections from twentieth-century writers of spiritual direction, writers whose work has provided countless thousands with encouragement, consolation and an informed understanding of the life of the spirit

Titles now available in the continuing series:

Thomas Merton
Metropolitan Anthony Bloom
Michael Ramsey
Rabbi Lionel Blue
Henri Nouwen
John Main
Carlo Carretto
Jean Vanier
Dietrich Bonhoeffer
Bede Griffiths